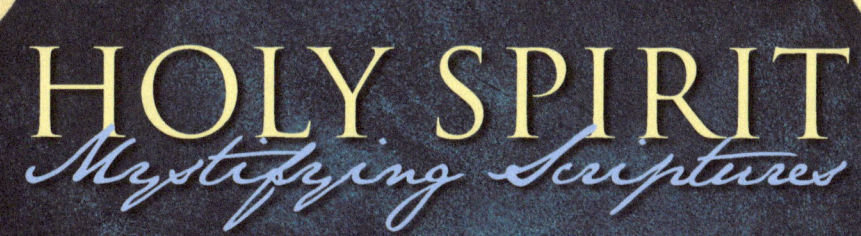

Primix Publishing
11620 Wilshire Blvd
Suite 900, West Wilshire Center, Los Angeles, CA, 90025
www.primixpublishing.com
Phone: 1-800-538-5788

© 2022 Carol J. Pitts. All rights reserved.

No part of this book may be reproduced, stored in a retrieval system, or transmitted by any means without the written permission of the author.

Published by Primix Publishing   04/20/2022

ISBN: 978-1-955177-70-2(sc)
ISBN: 978-1-955177-71-9(hc)
ISBN: 978-1-955177-72-6(e)

Library of Congress Control Number: 2021924945

Any people depicted in stock imagery provided by iStock are models, and such images are being used for illustrative purposes only.

Certain stock imagery © iStock.

Because of the dynamic nature of the Internet, any web addresses or links contained in this book may have changed since publication and may no longer be valid. The views expressed in this work are solely those of the author and do not necessarily reflect the views of the publisher, and the publisher hereby disclaims any responsibility for them.

A personal relationship with the Lord Jesus Christ

If you are viewing this book and do not know the Lord as your personal savior, I invite you to ask Him to forgive you of your sin's and then ask Him to come into your heart. He <u>will</u> come in and you <u>will</u> have a new start in life with a clean slate, you will be born again.

King James Version of the Bible

1 John 1:9 If we confess our sins, he is faithful and just to forgive us our sins and to cleanse us from all unrighteousness.

John 3:3 Jesus said, verily, verily, I say unto thee except a man (or woman) be born again, he cannot see the Kingdom of God.

John 3:16 For God so loved the world, that he gave his only begotten Son that whosoever believeth in him should not perish but have everlasting life.

*Now find a bible believing church and attend it. Your new Spirit will need the Word of God to grow.

Esther

Media: *Mixed*

Esther 2:7b

And he brought up Ha-das-sah, that is Esther, his uncle's daughter: for she had neither father nor mother and the maid was fair (*lovely*) and beautiful; whom morde'cai, when her father and mother were dead, took for his own daughter

(Esther was a natural beauty)
(Here she is her own description)

Her beauty was compared to the <u>flowers</u>.
Her skin was fair and the color of <u>sea shells</u>.
Her hair was shiny black like the jungle <u>leopard</u>.
Her lips were naturally red and sweet like the <u>apple</u>.
Her <u>eyes sparkled</u> and were <u>black as her hair</u>.
But her real <u>mark of beauty</u> was love,
and her <u>cup was full</u>.

The underlined items <u>are in</u> the painting.
** You will find the head of the leopard by the front of her forehead
The two curls of her hair are the front and back leg of the cat.
The cat's tail runs down the back of the painting.

A Caterpillar's Dream

A caterpillar's dream is to be on the wing
and she dreams her whole life through
that one day she'll soar from the grassy floor
through the trees up to the blue.

Then comes the day she must go away
for she knows her deaths cue,
so she inters her loom, sad at her doom
unaware that her dream will come true.

She's an earthbound worm about to learn
that dying brings beauty and wing
she'll emerge alive with wings to fly;
reborn a brand new thing.

Now she soars the sky, a butterfly,
a most wonders thing, she thinks.
A salute was due to God she knew,
So she gave the Lord a wink.

Thank you God she said with a nod
,for hearing my voice so small;
for the grass below…and for flowers to sow
and the days to ponder it all.
By Carol J. Pitts

Scripture 1

Death of His Saints

Media: *Mixed*

Psalms 116:15
Precious in the sight of the Lord
Is the death of his saints.

*This is a Word of Knowledge

*In the hands of Jesus is one of His deceased Spanish saints,
an angel holds a pillow under her head.
*After crossing the great divide (the dark blue) her now young Spirit enters
heaven and is greeted by a family member.

Scripture 2

A Fisher of Men

Media: *Digital*

Matt. 4:19
And he said unto them, Follow me, and I will make you fishers of men.

*She (a follower of Christ) prays to win souls to Christ in India.
The water jug in the painting has an elephant handle and has the look of India.
*The silly looking fish shows the Holy Spirit has a since of humor
and also says Christian.

Scripture 3

Even to Old Age

Media: *Digital*

Isa. 46:4
And even to your old age I *am* he;
and even to hoar (gray) hairs
will I carry you:

*This is a godly very elderly couple whom have
spent their life together in Christ.
*See the tears of love for the Lord in their eyes.

Scripture 4

Sing Praises

Media: *Digital*

Heb. 2:12b
Saying, in the midst of the church
will I sing praise unto thee.

*This is a look in the window of a small
country church at a young woman
worshiping God in song.*

Scripture 5

Praise the Lord in Dance

Media: *Digital*

Psalms 149:3a
Let them praise his name in dance:

---

*A Word of Knowledge
*This is a Japanese dancer worshiping
God in dance on a church stage
with a Christian audience.
*When you see the observer or person representing an audience note
that persons teeth are made by the dress of the dancer.

Scripture 6

A Prayer for Help

Media: *Digital*

Psalms 91:15

He shall call upon me, and I will answer him:
I will be with him in trouble; I will deliver him and honor him.

*This is a Christian man full of light in the jungle at night that appears to be
injured and is desperately praying for help while a leopard is upon him.
Answering his prayer, God subdued and closed the leopards' mouth.
  *The cat will not harm him.
  *See the <u>leopard</u> in black.
  *See the <u>lions</u> head in red in his head.
  **I believe this is a Word of Knowledge and actually happened.

Scripture 7

HE GIVES HIS BELOVED SLEEP

Media: *Digital*

Psalms 127:2b
For so he giveth his beloved sleep.

---

*Notice her hair, it's in the shape of a resting lamb.

Scripture 8

Power to Tread

Media: *Digital*

Psalms 127:2b
Behold, I give unto you power to tread on Serpents

*See Christian man, woman and youth shoes treading on the serpent.

Scripture 9

Before the Fall

Media: *Digital*

Gen. 2:24 (23 & 25)
Therefore shall a man leave his father
and mother and cleave unto
his wife: and they shall be one flesh.

*This is representatives of Adam and Eve with <u>love</u> in their eyes and clasp hands. Birds are friendly along with all the other animals not shown here.

Scripture 10

Fallen Mankind

Media: *Digital*

Gen. 3:8
… and Adam and his wife hid themselves
from the presents of the Lord God
amongst the trees of the garden.

*This is representatives of Adam and Eve
hiding among the trees from God for they had disobeyed Him. Notice the green leaf.
*Also look close you can see the serpent in Adam.
Their baby yet to be is seen between them in the light.*

Scripture 11

Youth Renewed like the Eagle's

Media: *Digital*

Psalms 103:5
Who satisfieth thy mouth with good things;
so that thy youth is renewed like the eagle's.

**You will find <u>two eagle</u> heads in his hair.
One white and the other multicolored.*

HOLY SPIRIT MYSTIFYING SCRIPTURES | 21

Scripture 12

My Hiding Place

Media: *Digital*

Psalms 119:114
*Thou art my hiding place and my shield;

*You will find the <u>face</u> of a hidden person in the representative of the Lord.
*The <u>shield</u> is the outline around the Lord.
*Evil spirits are on both sides of the <u>shield</u>.

Scripture 13

Creature Liberty

Media: *Digital*

Romans 8:21
Because the creature itself also shall be delivered from the bondage of corruption into the glorious liberty of the children of God.

Jesus and the Donkey

Media: *Digital*

Matt. 21:5b
Thy King cometh unto thee, meek, and sitting upon an ass, (*donkey*)

*Jesus when he rode into Jerusalem on the donkey was
speaking in picture language to the people who loved him.

*The picture said:
*See this gentle donkey I am sitting on, man has made this gentle beast a beast of burden.
He will soon carry a heavy load of man's cargo, just as I to will
soon carry man's heavy cargo load of sins on me.

*You will find the head, chest and arm of Jesus under the stripes on the tree.

Scripture 15

A Brawling Woman

Media: *Digital*

Proverbs 25:24
It is better to dwell in the corner of the housetop, than with a brawling woman.

*Take note of the woman's tongue,
She is <u>tongue lashing</u> the man.
*The colors in their hair, mainly hers
are the <u>colors</u> of the serpent, a carnal Woman.

Scripture 16

Worship in Spirit

Media: *Digital*

Matt. 11:28
…….. they that worship him
must worship him In Spirit and in truth.

*You will find the Holy Spirit in white bowing
over the male and female, whom are looking up in worship.*

Scripture 17

Moses

Media: *Mixed*

Deuteronomy 34:5-6
5. So Moses the servant of the Lord died there in the land of Moab, according to the word of the Lord.
6. And he buried him in a valley in the Land of Moab,

*Here we see him in a cliff crevice above the clouds.

Scripture 18

Salvation

Media: *Digital*

Luke 5:31-32
They that are whole need not a physician;
but they that are sick.
I came not to call the righteous, but sinners to repentance.

Scripture 19

A New Creature

Media: *Digital*

2 Cor. 5:17
Therefore if any man (*or woman*) be in Christ, he is <u>a new
Creature</u>: old things are passed away, behold,
all things have become new.

*See the New Creature.
*A butterfly is born anew, a different creature.

Scripture 20

Love thy God and Let Your Light Shine

Media: *Digital*

Mark 12:30
And thou shall love thy God with all thy heart,
and with all thy soul, and with all thy mind, and
with all thy strength: this is the first commandment.

Matt. 5:16
Let your light so shine before men,
that they may see your good works,
and glorify your father which is in heaven.

*This painting reads: (fish) Christian, love your
God with all your heart, soul and mind
and let your little light shine.

HOLY SPIRIT MYSTIFYING SCRIPTURES

Scripture 21

The Garden Lost

Media: *Digital*

Gen. 3:17
And unto Adam he said,
Because thou hast harkened unto the
voice of thy wife, and hast eaten of the tree,
of which I commanded thee, Thou shalt not eat of it:
cursed is the ground for thy sake; in sorrow
shall thou eat of it all the days of thy life

*See the expression on Adams face and on Eve's face,

Scripture 22

POWER OF PRAYER

Media: *Mixed*

Matt.6:6
But thou, when thou prayest, enter into thy closet, and when thou hast shut thy door, pray to thy Father which is in secret; and thy Father which seeth in secret shall reward thee openly.

---

*A Word of Knowledge to the power of prayer.
*Here the Holy Spirit is nailing the demon to the wall in chains, in answer to prayer and you can see the demon under the chains.

Scripture 23

A Woman's Glory

Media: *Digital*

1 Cor. 11:15
But if a woman has long hair, it is a glory to her:
for her hair is given her for a covering.

―⁕―

The painting speaks for its self.

Scripture 24

Come Unto Me

Media: *Digital*

Matt. 11:28
Come unto me, all ye that labor and
are heavy laden, and I will give you rest.

*The scripture and painting say it all.

Scripture 25

BURIED WITH HIM

Media: *Mixed*

Romans 6:4
Therefore we are buried with him by baptism into death:
that like as Christ was raised up from the dead by
the glory of the father, even so we also should walk in newness of life.

**The painting is a headstone at the head of a grave,
as well as the entrance to
a new road to travel, walk in newness of life.*

The Chosen

Matt. 22:14

Scripture 26

The Chosen

Media: *Mixed*

Matt. 22:14
For many are called, but few are chosen.

The painting represents all the chosen.
("It Reads")
They
are full of Light
with the mind of Christ the Lamb
and they see through the Eyes of the Holy Spirit, the Dove.

52 | CAROL J. PITTS

Scripture 27

Fight the Good Fight

Media: *Digital*

1 Tim. 6:12
Fight the good fight of faith, lay hold on eternal life,
Where,unto thou art also called, …………

---

*He has slain the old man (old nature) with a two <u>edged sword</u>, the (Word of God), and is going forth with the word and the <u>Breastplate of Righteousness.</u>

Scripture 28

Redeemed

Media: *Digital*

1 Peter 1:18

Forasmuch as ye know that ye were not redeemed with Corruptible things, as silver and gold, from your vain conversation received by tradition from your fathers; but with the precious blood of Christ, as of a lamb without blemish and without spot:

---

*The painting speaks for itself.

Scripture 29

When I was a Child

Media: *Digital*

1 Cor. 13:11
When I was a Child, I spake as a child,
I understood as a child, I though as a child:
But when I became a man (*or woman*),
I put away childish things.

*The form of a child's face can be found in her hair.

Scripture 30

Jesus the Lamb Lifted Up

Media: *Mixed*

John 3:14
And as Moses lifted up the serpent in the wilderness,
even so must the Son of man be lifted up:

**Jesus had to be <u>lifted up on the cross</u>
and die in order for <u>His spirit to enter men's
and women's heart's</u> and save them from their sin's.*

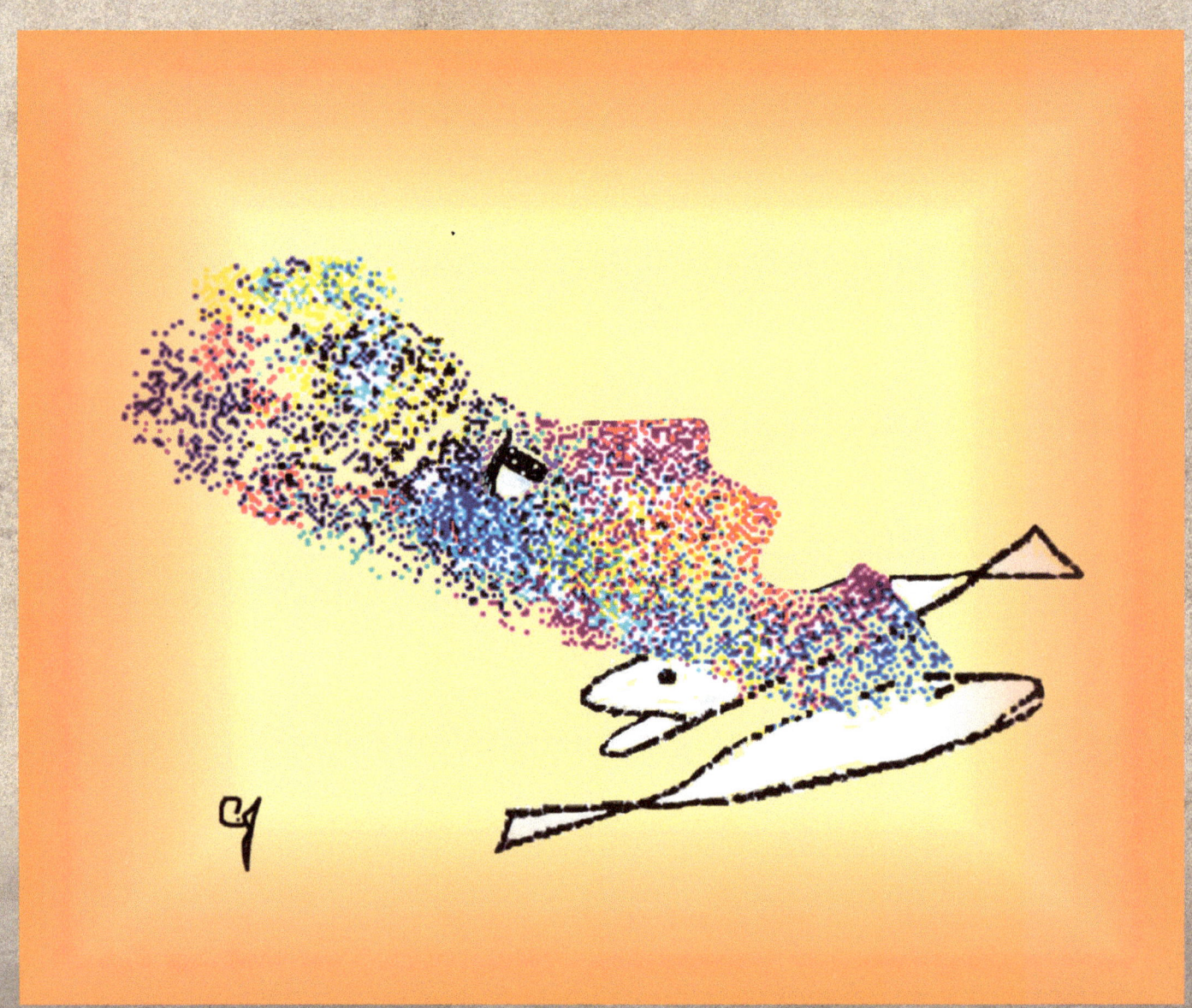

Scripture 31

Preacher

Media: *Digital*

Romans 10:14b
And how shall they hear without a preacher?

**See the face of the preacher
and the souls that are saved (the two fish) by
hearing the Word of God.*

Scripture 32

As a Little Child

Media: *Digital*

Mark 10:15
Verily I say unto you, whosoever shall not receive the kingdom of God
As a little child, he shall not enter therein.

*She sees the light of salvation and with tears she accepts her savior.

Scripture 33

Before the Throne

Media: *Digital*

Heb. 4:16
Let us boldly come unto the throne of grace,
that we may obtain mercy and find grace to help
in times need.

*The curtains form the throne
*Within is the throne room

Scripture 34

He Gives His Beloved Sleep

Media: *Digital*

Psalms 127:2b
Fore so He giveth his beloved sleep.

---

*Notice her hair, it's in the form of a resting lamb.

Scripture 35

Jesus Prays Love in the Spirit

Media: *Digital*

Matt.14:23

And when he had sent the multitudes away, he went up in a mountain apart to pray: and when the evening was come, he was there alone.

"This is a Word of Knowledge"

The head of Jesus is bent down, at the left in His beard is a <u>heart shape</u> and over to the right from the heart is His mouth and out of His mouth you can see prayer coming out, next is His nose and the slit is His eye.

Scripture 36

Holy Ghost Baptism with Fire

Media: *Digital*

Matt.3:11
I indeed baptize you with water unto repentance; but He that cometh after me is mightier than I: He shall baptise you with the Holy Ghost and fire.

"This is a Word of Knowledge"

The head of Jesus is bent down, at the left is a heart shape and over to the right is His mouth and out of His mouth you can see prayer coming out, next is His nose and the slit is His eye.

www.ingramcontent.com/pod-product-compliance
Lightning Source LLC
Chambersburg PA
CBHW040001290426
43673CB00077B/292